ANOTHER SUNSET
WE SURVIVE

ANOTHER SUNSET
WE SURVIVE

KATE GRAY

CEDAR HOUSE BOOKS

For permission to reproduce selections
from this book, contact
Cedar House Books
PO Box 3323
Friday Harbor, WA 98250
gt@cedarhousebooks.org

Cover art: Emily Carr, *Young Pines and Sky*, c. 1935,
oil on paper, 88.8 x 58.2 cm,
Collection of the Vancouver Art Gallery, Emily Carr Trust,
VAG 42.3.80, Photo: Trevor Mills, Vancouver Art Gallery
Book design: Beth Spencer
Author photograph: Lorre Jaffe

ISBN: 978-0-9635727-8-3
Library of Congress Control Number: 2007925865

what we know,
what we do

Acknowledgments

The author gratefully acknowledges the editors of the following magazines and anthologies in which these poems have appeared:

Born Magazine: "If the Only Heading is North"
Calyx: "Another Sunset We Survive"
Eclipse: "*Bastante*," "Dear Sir, Comma"
In the Arms of Words: Poems for Disaster Relief: "The Moon on the Tsunami"
Knowing Stones: Poems of Exotic Places: "Sulawesi"
Mid-American Review: "On September 12, I Can't Stop"
North American Review: "Turquoise Lies"
The Portland Light Anthology: "Catch and Release"
Rock & Sling: "Ploughshares," "The Silence of Moonlight"
South Dakota Review: "Long Row on Hatches Pond"

The following poems appeared in *Where She Goes* published by Blue Light Press, 2000: "Catch and Release," "Lantern," "Beginning with the Bang," "The Loneliest Part," and "Where She Goes."

The following poems appeared in *Bone-Knowing*, a chapbook published by Gertrude Press, 2006: "Unlike Other Exiles," "Catch and Release," "The Frame of Memory," "A Crown for a Rebel Cousin," "Lantern," "This Spring," "*Bastante*," and "If the Only Heading is North."

My immense gratitude to the Oregon Literary Arts Council, the communities at Hedgebrook and Norcroft and Soapstone, to Colleen McElroy, Sharon Hashimoto, the ODDs, Diane Averill, the Dangerous Writing community, Adrianne Wesol, Nan Collie, and most of all, to Cheryl Hollatz-Wisely, the one of a kind, the river.

TABLE OF CONTENTS

LONG ROW ON HATCHES POND   13

SISTER, I SAW   14

ON SEPTEMBER 12, I CAN'T STOP   16

UNLIKE OTHER EXILES   17

CATCH AND RELEASE   19

A CROWN FOR A REBEL COUSIN   20

WHAT POETS DO   27

TO NAME THE STARS   28

PLOUGHSHARES   33

BASTANTE   34

WHERE SHE GOES   35

RARELY ANYMORE DO I WAKE MYSELF CALLING   36

THE FOREST TURNS   37

THE FRAME OF MEMORY   38

TO A FRIEND RETURNING TO A LOVER FOR THE NINTH TIME   40

UNDER THE TONGUE   41

BEGINNING WITH THE BANG   42

WITH OUR HANDS   43

THE LONELIEST PART   44

SNAKE DANCE   45

THE SILENCE OF MOONLIGHT   47

DEAR SIR, COMMA   49

Hand-me-down   53

Sulawesi   55

Veni, Vidi, Vici   56

If the Only Heading Is North   57

Elegy for Kippy Liddle at Twenty-Three   58

Let Go the Thread   59

Turquoise Lies   60

Lantern   62

Some Sign   63

Someplace Safe   65

Something To Wear   67

The Moon on the Tsunami   68

Another Sunset We Survive   70

This Spring   73

What is to give light must endure burning.

~Viktor Frankl

LONG ROW ON HATCHES POND

At sunset all trees turned liquid, bark shimmering
like fish scales. Steep hills of pine sloped

into the lake; trees grew close. Branches dark
and interlocking kept me off shore. Near a pine

knocked down, I cast a lure for a wide-mouth
bass to bite. Few did. Still I rowed the old

metal boat far from the abandoned shack, the dock,
the landing where birches gathered. At the far end

reeds sprung cattails. Redwing blackbirds bristled
warnings. After one enormous pull I tucked

the oars like wings, hurled my raw body headlong
into the bow, arms stretching over gunwales, chest

pressing the ridge, my nose nearly plowing into water.
I parted lily pads, flew low through a forest of weeds

until I thudded but did not tip. Rolling to face the sky
darkening, my seat on the hull, legs draped over bench,

I heard the thick crickets trill the night, truce
from stifling day. Then wind came to drag me home.

Sister, I Saw

My sister hoarded smoke, the reek of charred wood dowsed
by water and damned, the smell was one of the few
things living after flames took our room, so
she sealed it in a black vinyl bag made
for doll clothes. She tucked it deep
inside a closet in our new home, dug
it out when she thought I slept as if
smell could not break
sleep. Smoke never
leaves. It enters
everything
and never
washes out.

The round bag, laid on the crisscross of her legs, she unzipped
one tooth at a time. As the tab traveled across
the plastic track, she lost years
from her face. Eight years old
again, her eyes did not
shift. They filled with
dolls she lost, laughter
of aunts and uncles,
all eyes on her.
Blonde curls
in bows she
danced.

Then at fifteen she bossed and bothered, knocked boys
over, embarrassing me. I did not see her spread
the bag apart, the way a Bible might
open on to John, the witness,
the writer. I heard her
breathe. And with
those breaths
she let out
all she
could
not
tell.

ON SEPTEMBER 12, I CAN'T STOP

staring at one businessman falling headfirst
from the tower. His arms and legs do not paw
the air. He is not a kite with his tie a tail.
He is more missile than man, his head the dome
and trigger, his body a titanium shell, just as vivid, just
as dumb. Now I know the clammy hold of images, why
the eye flickered and bulged in the broken window
of the college locker room years ago where I showered
in a different man's gaze. And it is the calm of this man
urging me to stare over and over, the magnified shot
of his face, his eyes watching the unrepentant street,
the approach of a terrible body, its greeting
a shattering. I can't leave him. In his descent
I finger a slick, clean fear and a grace
so fierce it whistles like a bomb.

UNLIKE OTHER EXILES

1.

He melted down to twigs, a nose, and shriveled eyes.
He called funeral homes and their evasions tasted grainy,
a paste made from betrayal. Each refused
his remains. Everyone he knew when whole had died
the same, the body first betrayed, then the mind, then
the spirit, a trinity decayed. On a San Francisco street
he found an empty can, a string, so he called the line.

2.

She volunteered to hold the other end
of lives. The thrum of passing
pain from mouth to mouth. She listened to
men open fear, scrape dreams
from cans and eat advice, each voice
sounding more wind than syllable,
like this man no one would bury,
his blood venom to embalmers.
In all of San Francisco only two
funeral homes took bodies desiccated
by AIDS. He talked T-cells,
drugs, and what his transparent skin
revealed. She was all that was left,
capillaries like fan coral. Without graves
she wondered where gays went and what
marked their land. She read off names,
numbers, knowing he would be such dust.

3.

Despite years of looking she could find nothing of her mother except
bird feeders without seed and bamboo tapping. After the divorce
her mother had fallen for a slap-fisted man and disappeared.
Police stumped, neighbors blind as root balls, she searched
journals, bars, ports like San Francisco, found loss marked
in men's flesh. AIDS passed with notice, a cause few could miss.
At least she could touch death on the phone by talking to dying
men. She could be with a people different from other exiles
because they had no earth to bury dead. She had no dead to bury.

CATCH AND RELEASE

Just past boathouses south of Ross Island, flashes
of struggle showed a fish caught firm. Silver shards
broke thin skins of water. Yesterday my friend's brother
died that way. Like a greedy sea lion, AIDS batted him back
and forth, broke eardrums, pierced jawbone, stripped
flesh from ribs. Before the end when seizures were sure signs
nerves still worked, his body like divers arching
into back-dives plummeted, flopping him flat-backed
on sweat-stained beds, splashed him with
　　spasms, shocks, regrets. Only when family arrived
did nurses let him swim in valium. Yesterday doctors, fishers
of empty shells, unhooked him from tubes, let him go
dead. All I can do today is resist the slap of water passing
and back through shifting currents with a brittle bow.

A Crown for a Rebel Cousin

1.

Maid of honor this good dyke does not make
but thank you for the thought: I'll wear
my purple tux or, with sleeves rolled up, prepare
a toast comparing you to Joan, the one who staked
everything on words she heard in clouds.
I've seen you read the sky: "Shadows on the hill
never find a home, always drift until
they pluck melodies on trees, tunes played loud
by God," you whined, a twelve-year-old cross
between prissy girl and Pegasus. Thank God
you now write unlike you scanned the sky!
You cleared fences fast and tossed
reins, rode bareback, discerned words lost
to tongues. Not resigned, you grew defiant.

2.

You tongued defiant words, opted not to malign
our family's roots. Like berry seeds, stubborn tears
lodged behind the teeth you clenched because you feared
showing faults. So like buried bones, benign
growths surfaced in malignant signs
of love, burrowing through your breast
the wormy dreams of harboring Daddy's best
girl. You, best cousin, are neither servant
nor host to any man. Once you asked
me to bless premarital sex at seven-
teen when to me, most naive, sex sounded
big, bigger than any secrets passed around
the girls' locker room. At eighteen all sins
chip the Catholic lacquer off a mask.

3.

We chipped the Catholic lacquer off our masks,
took jackhammers to our faces. Religion
soaked our pores, made our heroines nuns
in every tale. When will our mothers' pasts
not jerk our hands? Our fathers went to Yale,
our mothers golfed, bore six kids, ate boiled eggs,
lust as sweet as penance. My verses begged
the simpleness of Psalms. I could not rail
too loud, hail "Christ," put skin to skin without
cringing from its friction—my makeup strips out
what I've made of myself, and like you,
Priscilla, I have moved. Our differences grew
with distances culled from dreams our mothers
never had. I also had a lover.

4.

My mother never dreamed I'd have a lover,
I called her Chip and kissing her, splintered
like Duchamp's "Nude Descending," wintered
hopes of reaching God, Man, and other-
wise, Yale. Confessing sin I told you first,
love never means the gloss
of saying "sorry, wrong sex" or possibly
"I do." I did expect to hear our mothers' worst
from your lips—"That's gross!"—instead
you said, "That's love." For me you wove
a tapestry to catch and wrap the unsaid
stones, those we sank in riverbeds overflowing
without sound. Now with three all-night bands,
you vow your life to a Turkish-born Frenchman.

5.

A lifetime with a French director, a man
whose eyes tell stories in foreign tongues—
unsung tales: a woman's *bildungsroman*,
an *homme fatal*, a single father-in-tran-
sition. With him, you'll dress the Rue de Victor
Hugo in orange cat, green velvet yard, and piano
taps to dance his son through throes
of growing pains. You ached in Florence
when statues shaped your longing
for children in the way water wears
on rock, washes like the falls
of Sages Ravine, smoothing and speeding the bare
pulse of earth. You learned your curves belonged
in a sculptor's hands, who'd sell your statue to malls.

6.

Your statue stands dead-center in a mall
in Saskatchewan. Shoppers never pause
enough to connect this art with the girl once awed
by colts and clouds. Clay figures do not fall
for bearded men, laughter across an ocean, prayer
or half-sung chants by ancient people
pushed from ancestral homes. Here under steeple
and synagogue you will wrap your ways
of wandering in cloth our mothers wove
from clover and silk, the family lines spun
by our hands. Together you will shape a life
of art. Chopin, Shakespeare, Ibsen, Stein striving
to elevate the ordinary and make stunning
the conundrums of becoming husband and wife.

7.

Conundrums make the lives of husbands and wives
extraordinary, historical. You two bridge
the gaps of Jews and Catholics, of mother languages,
of content fitting form. Together you'll survive
genealogy, disease, and scorn. The wagers
will be placed on differences dividing you.
Our family does not know that root values
of the love you make hold no gauge,
no science, only art. The power to awaken
dream, to read the trees or hear shadows
playing melodies on hills is strength
you must hide, Priscilla, behind armor as old
as Joan of Arc's. She was pushed to great lengths.
What a good dyke she might have made.

WHAT POETS DO
~for Sharon Hashimoto

Only a poet sorts *grief*—
a riptide shredding
bodies on rocks—from
mourning—bones
rolled by surf.

I can just see you
flat-backed at
your desk, salt-and-pepper hair
straight like rain from storm clouds
in the desert at Manzanar where
your mother jump-roped
for years inside barbed wire
hung on stripped-pine poles, fencing
your kind. She didn't talk
about it, so little
either of you said.

Now a week after
her death, you stare
at the yellow tablet, weighing
words, your right hand resting
the pen, your left hand
on your cat, Cirrus, the cloud,
the herald of bad weather. You are
the one in the family who holds
the mirror for us all, much like
your mother held
the mirror for you to see
her reflection in your face. No
wonder your hands are still.

To Name the Stars

Chlorine rose from concrete floor
of the bath house, slats
in the changing room lousy
with mold. My bones cold after I rode
to the poolhouse at one o'clock the night
the Bicentennial brought the whole town
to fireworks in our backyard.

*

Earlier that evening deep
in pachysandra, you stripped
and straddled Chris Hunter. Booze
and nothing better to do drew you
to him. We both hated his hair
oozing down his back, pimples
like sumac on his cheeks, and later

when I heard you moan, "No,"
through the dark powder air
between my bedroom, your bedroom, our mother's
empty room, I burst through the door.
Naked, your boobs at bad angles,
you yelled, "Go away." I said,
with my arm out, an archer's arm,
"Chris, get the fuck out of my
mother's house." My first
swear word, it flew
from my throat like sparks.

The front door slammed, engine revved,
you soon stampeded my room: "Don't tell."

*

In minutes I clicked the kickstand, wheeled
down the road under no moon, the canopy
of oak and elm opening to light I could now name.
Cassiopeia, her crown an offering. Scorpio,
its red star throbbing from Orion's fight. Lyra,
like a dolphin arcing by the cross. No night owl,
no bat, just the grumble of tires and brake screech.

Miles away the open poolhouse offered
plastic curtains on metal rings, hot, hot water
shuddering, and stalls to hold my body
still loud and ringing like Orion's sword.

PLOUGHSHARES

There can be no feeling like it, the sword
in two hands, the head suspended, no motion
like the lift of another body on a blade, a cord
cut by a religious man, a man clothed in devotion.

His two hands suspend a head, the motion
skipping in video, internet streaming, colors mute,
the cleric cuts after words of distortion
read above a kneeling, blindfolded, orange-suited

man on video-streaming internet, whose prayers are mute
to the whole world watching. He knows. We know
the image now, the kneeling, blindfolded, orange-suited
man losing his head. The first, Nick Berg, showed

us brutality unknown, in hand. Now we know
the lift of another body on the blade, a cord
in the head severed, like Nick Berg, the peepshow.
There can be no feeling like this sword.

BASTANTE

The last time I was a man, I sliced olives
and spread each green butterfly
on his tongue so he would know salt.

The time before that, I climbed the branches
of mango trees to pick soft globes and slip slices
on his tongue so he would know sunlight.

The time before that time, I pinched mint leaves,
crushed fistfuls in my palms, ran them along
the sinews of his neck, so he would know cold.

The next time I am a man, I will crush chipotle
between stones, dust my fingers and taste each one,
kiss his lips lightly, so he will know fire.

When I am a man, my name is *Bastante*. The world
I reach gives my hands enough to touch, shows me
what my skin knows, the taste of believing.

Where She Goes

On the river rowing blind, all I really know
is her voice, its tone and thickness consistent as
blood flowing through veins. In the double scull
she tells me when to risk, how to jump at "Attention,
Go," to push through pain of breathing without
air. Each a Ruth for the other, we drive away
some women's warnings: we will bulge,
be muscle-bound. Last weekend she guided me
through tests on rowing machines, air
sucked and measured through tubes, blood
tapped evenly. Better than a cox'n, she called,
"Long and strong," and afterwards
cooling down on the glide, I came close
to knowing what faith entails. It is
her words that wake me to sights
rarely seen: the way currents lace up
river from the Sellwood Bridge, how buoys
mislead, how surely water marks stone, wood,
and flesh. With words like gifts of grain,
she showed me how to trust the fullness
of four oars pulling as one.

Rarely Anymore Do I Wake Myself Calling

After my father slipped from my room
sometimes my voice chafed
like branches in the wind.
My mother never heard.

Sometimes in late afternoon after he put me down
for a nap, I tried to lift my hands
to my mouth, curl my fingers, one hand in the other
the way calla lilies form
a tube, to boom my mother's name.
But I couldn't.
And she didn't hear.

Year after year I kept quiet, growing
around my silence the way pine bark
folds barbed wire in its skin.

THE FOREST TURNS

On the Maple Trail in the thick
of Forest Park, yellow tape flaps. Rough
two-by-fours painted white, a cross leans
from the dry V of a riverbed. Candles
in tall cylinders, the type used to light
graves on *El Dia de los Muertos*, tip
like drunks on each other. I remember
the shots of helicopters chopping overhead
while boy scouts bent shoulder to shoulder
in brush to find clues, a tear of cloth, a pair
of glasses. He must have been big,
the reporters mused, to have carried
each woman up the steep slope. The big man
huffed his way uphill, dumped three bodies.
He had to have parked at the place
I have parked for years to walk my dogs.

Through blackberries grabbing the path few use
after news reports, I pick my way, walk out
of brambles into woods, enter a sudden
silence buried between canopy and
undergrowth, a fold in the labia of these hills
where little wind and little light reach, nothing stirs
at the edge of murder. Under oak and alder
over salal and fern, I feel the forest turn
to vault. The spirits of three women
meet peacefully, speak softly, touch clothes
never again to be torn. They are veins
running in bark with soft rain. They are ferns
springing from fallen logs. They are cedars rising
from the same root, connected in death
as never in life, three women at rest
in the opening of cool hard shade.

THE FRAME OF MEMORY

~at the opening of the United States Holocaust Memorial
Museum, Washington, D.C., 1993

We sent prayers silent as crows gliding overhead, spirits
drawn to dusk, and placed pink carnations in a triangle on the lawn
making the *rosa Winkel*, the pink badge the Nazis sewed
on homosexuals. From the outside, the window
of clear glass frame and opaque panes over the entrance marked
the way everything became its shadow: the frame let light in,
the glass darkened. The evening buckled with the suck
of candles stuck through styrofoam, cups to catch wax, the singe
of flame starting a stream of candlelight through a crowd.
We shook with each name pronounced, men and women
we had never read about in school or print, a rumor whispered

    Friedrich Althoff

years ago as if we heard it wrong, five to fifteen thousand
homosexuals gassed for "lewd and lascivious acts."

    Eric Langer

This crowd of sun-scorched men and women
marching on the Mall was the first
in history to call the names out loud,

    August Pfeiffer

the many names turning on tongues, dust
to blood red bone. With each candle raised in ritual
we faced the limestone mantle of sixteen panes, the building
with room for horror and sadness, meant to grip
the visitor so tightly that each body feels more
than it can stand. Memory stretches sinew into the future.

38

Gays killed because they dared waste Aryan seed, would not
bear Aryan babies. Their ashes frame the irony of our past.

   Lilly Schragenheim

Once pinned with pink triangles, they perished.
Because they were slaughtered, they live on.
They are the only dead we can identify, whose gassed
and ghostly bodies we claim, whose lives resonate
in the walls of one of the few museums in the world
to call us by name.

To a Friend Returning to a Lover for the Ninth Time

Salmon do
the same, dying
each leap up
the dam. Hummingbirds
return to the same
red rhodie, trill wings
and tickle blossoms
with their liquid
bills. Each cycle
you say, "This time is
different." You say,
"But I love her," as if
your love is lava, the earth's
first secretion, somehow
sacrosanct. You say,
"We've grown," and all
I can say is I've grown
tired.

UNDER THE TONGUE
~for Stevan after reading "Convert" by Paulann Petersen

For three days a writer crossed his legs
in his crimson dress and sat under
the rhododendrons, their pompom blossoms sprung.
While his wife and sons were busy about their farm
in Estacada, he drew down his skirt
over the hair of his thighs, one hand patting
the strands of his ponytail. The honey he sucked
through his Ruby Supreme lips pooled
until clumped, it plunged
under his tongue.

Hummingbirds, their vermillion bodies
dolphin-dancing on his chin and cheek,
dipped in him, and now
his every word
shudders.

BEGINNING WITH THE BANG

Science has made much ado about sex but reduced the mystery to
"the union of gametes producing zygotic cells." Still, practice made
theories, and Freud and Kinsey agreed on the bottom
line that bodies and minds intertwine. On larger scales
some might say the universe began with physical
attraction: some celestial body drew in masses of molecules, and
KABLOOEY—we banged into space. But the 1990s erupt
in a different fashion. Researchers try to unravel science
from sex. They want The Big Bang renamed. Without adventure
they try titles like *Early Gas Altering Development* (EGAD), or
without accuracy, *Wild Oscillation of Worlds* (WOW), or without anything
The First Explosion. They believe they can keep mystery out
of language, their new name staying put like a planet, but words
walk through time unsteadily carrying their meanings, dropping
suggestive pieces and holding others tight.

So, no matter what we name it, what you and I began
was big. It happened with a shift not a bang. When we met,
my molecules fused, and I experienced evolution: my lungs filled
with air, not water, and instead of slithering, I now stand. Our words,
like nebulae condensing and separating, form worlds. With hands
passing from breasts to hearts, we try to hold what we cannot grasp.

With Our Hands

Near the houses where we lived separately
and loved, the hawk spotted prey and plunged
wing-tucked, blue-brown streaks in its crown,
red eyes blurred before it slammed into glass.

Now slumped in grass, its head dangling, it lay
with breast puffed, tail bright with brown bands.
When you led me to the dead hawk, your eyes
shone like moons waning, the light

a type of dying. And we could not speak.
We hovered the way my aunt and I bent
years ago above a grouse she shot. "Look,"
she said above the quivering bird, "you must

break its neck with your hands. It's cruel
to let birds suffer." Above the broken hawk
we wished our hands could rend our hearts
still rapt in love, or else, for flight restored.

The Loneliest Part

of sculling is the hands released from
    the body, floating above
    the thighs, then in the slow ride
    up the slide waiting, waiting like
    a moonrise before dropping
    oars into pooling water, before
    catching fire on the drive.

of sex is lips released from
    lips, letting a lover shudder in her own
    world, her quaking quieting as you
    rise to cover breasts with breasts, before
    breathing blends the bodies.

of living is letting go the hold
    of pain, the cool smooth flesh of the pet
    boa wrapped around the throat, the familiar
    weight, the scent of scales, the certain
    constriction until you raise the noose
    above your head, before
    you breathe freely and fill your lungs with

the loneliness you miss.

SNAKE DANCE

One sister's hand
a snake's mouth,
flat flesh un-
hinged, pinned
my other sister's neck
to wall and timber.

It was years before
the horn's wild notes drew
the snake away, before
I slit and sucked
the wounds.

In the spit I spit before
us all, we sisters saw
the vituperation
of our father's sperm,
his words, his insane
work, what he forced
down throats, how
he bid the older
dance and strike,
the younger squirm,
all glory his.

But even now
the charm reigns
without the charmer.
A type of rage raises
its false face, the hood's two eyes
painted in scales
still takes
my voice, and I

cannot act, and I
cannot pull
away.

THE SILENCE OF MOONLIGHT

Frozen so fast
        weeds caught waving
the ice glinted in the moonlight
        six feet thick
beneath a full moon
        skates carving crazy shapes
white on black ice
        like chalkboard scribbling
        like an ancient alphabet.

She was alone
        on the big lake,
        the deepest lake in Connecticut,
five miles from a home
        crowded with siblings and secrets,
        black marks etched before she was born:
                her mother's binges
                her father's rage.
She turned and spun and
        flung out her arms
        as if the arc of her arms were the curve
        of the world.

She was Atlas holding heavens on her shoulders
        spiraling beneath the planets,
        the plans of her family
                to turn her staid and married,
                to raise her Anglican like her father
                        and nobody else,

but for a moment she breathed the way Atlas breathed
    when Hercules took the world.

Her body soaring over the lake
skating in solitude
        the silence of gods and moonlight,
        her slate slick and clean
as she sliced the quick black ice
before slinging skates by their laces
        and shouldering her way home.

DEAR SIR, COMMA

Sometimes folding my body like origami to hide
under my mother's vanity, I held my breath
when she entered the room.
Other times I feigned
weightlessness to walk
over creaky New England floors and sat
outside the bathroom where she soaked
in Jean Naté, heard the plop of bright balls
of oil in hot, hot water.
Sometimes from my room
I heard her voice, tired
from raising six children
in the '60s, tired
from hacking herself away
from my father rooting
his madness in us all.

Her job was answering the mail
for her brother, a pundit
launching conservative reform in language
and politics. Enunciating into a microphone,
the tape taking her voice in tight rounds
to a secretary in an office in New York City,
my mother's open syllables turned.
My grandfather had trained her Os
and As. From my room I heard her
answer the letters squabbling
over my uncle's columns, "Dear Sir
Comma My Cap brother
appreciates your concern
Period," punctuating my sleep.

Now nearly forty, I hear my mother's voice
long-distance, the lilting tone, the training
of faintly British vowels. Working my job,
responding to compositions by students
who do not hear words parried in political debate,
I speak into a computer, my voice springing into type.
I hear my round vowels, "Dear Student, Comma,"
and I see my mother bent above her desk.

kg

HAND-ME-DOWN

An azalea of a woman, my grandmother quickened
in spring, her staircase a waterfall of wisteria,
garden pools flush with goldfish, lilacs and magnolias
as lavish as stories told by Irish living in the South.
My mother was born a Yankee, content
before a winter's fire. One March she herded us south,
drove over raked gravel in the driveway to downtown
Camden, South Carolina, the white part, shaded
by trees and department stores in the 1960s. New
to big stores and youngest of six, I lived
in soft clothes, elbows bowed. Inheritance
smelled like hand-me-downs.

We were going out. I needed clothes, my mother
announced and marched me into a starched store.
For a big girl, taller than boys my age, the first
dress I saw was orange, the color of sun and sweetness
and all things not New England. With a big box
I jumped back in the car, rode over red-dirt roads
where black women walked in white shoes.

That evening seven of us piled into the car and followed
the Cadillac carrying my grandmother to Big Red's house.
This Irish lawyer boasted that years ago piano jazz had drawn him
through the woods to find the musician who could not see. "He cannot read
a note," Big Red called to his guests, and the piano man flashed
a full smile, playing rhythms for those who did not tap
or dance but took them to be a sign the South would rise again.

After hours of listening, I swelled in my orange dress.
I jabbed my older sister, doubled back my thumbs,
and sighed. When the piano man struck notes of "Dixie," a

woman poked me with her cane. "Get up, you damn Yankee,"
she boomed a thunder of whiskey, and we six sprang.
The adults had stood and with one voice sang except six damn
Yankees staring at our mother who suddenly could drawl.

SULAWESI

On the island of Sulawesi, mothers
    with machetes cut tombs in tree trunks,
ebony, mahogany. In hibiscus they hollow a place for bodies
    dead from drinking water, river water
stagnating, soil saturated, nothing stays buried
    on land. They place small bodies upright
in graves carved in the heart of wood, lash bark doors
    shut with sashes until they seal, faint green lines marking
casket covers in trees. In the rainforests of Sulawesi
    trees sway in the hot breeze, each marked
with latchless doors. They rock small wooden hearts.

VENI, VIDI, VICI

They could take the world. Start close,
their home town, St. Petersburg, soon
Tampa, then they could spread like spring.
They could fill swamps, disguise
themselves as storms. Take the Tallahassee,
the Shenandoah, rise up through edges
of ice. In Blue Ridge Mountains they might ooze
like sap or bloom like dogwood, in Ozarks rut like
skunks through sod. Through desert grass they'd gallop
over northern New Mexico. They'd take the Rockies like
a sudden thaw ripping down moraines. Across the continent
they'd melt rivers like the Charles, flood the St. Lawrence. Canada
would fall in a day. Mexico would lead to song and they'd sing
through Ecuador, the Amazon, and shout where great oceans clash.

One with cancer, one with HIV, together they laugh like tulips bursting.
Neither girl has loved like this. At twenty, they will not outlive their plan:
dominate the world with passion. But for a time, they love like Caesar.

IF THE ONLY HEADING IS NORTH

on my compass
and the compass I palm
is your body
and I ignore the moss markings
in the forest,
then suddenly
cedar branches sprout
needles around their spine
like spruce,
and spruce sprout
stocking caps that flop
like hemlock.
I turn circles
into the brown knot
of your eyes,
my lips tracking
blond edges
of your brown
knotted hair.
Pointing my needle
to your true north,
following only
the quivering force
in my palm
to find my way,
leads me
sixteen degrees
off.

ELEGY FOR KIPPY LIDDLE AT TWENTY-THREE

Her oar slapped us, backed us through walls
some girls learn. She was our guide
to powers girls combine, as all

eight rowers jumped high at her call
to pass pain by, to find our fears denied.
She slapped us, backed us through false walls,

the isolating words, the feeble notions we fall
prey to. With taut muscles, we did not hide
the power eight combined when "ready-all"

we rowed. If we broke, we stalled
the steady run, the dreams of women riding
the slap of strokes that backed us through the walls,

the rough waters women are to skirt or crawl
within. Trusting in the glide, she widened
the power eight of us believed all

women everywhere, willing to stand tall,
will use to show our strength, not hide
our power. To take the risks set all

eight minds. In every stroke, our doubts dispelled.
We leapt to follow Kippy's lead. Her glide
and slap of oar steered the boat against the tide.
Steadily she backed us through the wall

to love, the power she left us all.

LET GO THE THREAD
~in response to William Stafford's "The Way It Is"

My hold on that thread has kept
New England close, leaves composting
to lace, sap popping like buckshot,
daffodils breaking snow. Your Kansas
and my Connecticut tug their ends.

But I don't want to stop time's unfolding.
The camellia bud, its spiral whirling open, unleashing
the bloody bloom of all my father wrecked, now
drops, turns to sod. His hand
in my underwear, his thick impregnable
fingers, unplugged the Yankee reluctance:
I've become a poet, and testified.

Luke, when he wrote about lepers, thought
ungrateful the nine not prostrating before Jesus.
Maybe they knew mercy meant they could walk on,
that leprosy and healing struck a balance, the way fires
cleanse a forest. Maybe their bones knew
their skin melting was as divine
as flesh made whole, transmutable.

Letting go to know change, the way it is fraught
with boils and scars, the way it slips
under the wet palm and sticks to the wet
thigh. If you let go the thread, behold the present
flesh and praise the way it is.

TURQUOISE LIES

Blue and unwinking, your eyes scared me, and the lies
you told when we were kids flowed freely like drinks
poured every evening, five o'clock sharp. Our family's art
was mixing pity and piety in religion and politics, writing
about purity while plying wine. You, sweet cousin, painted
masterpieces in water and words but couldn't wipe away pain.

Your body, denied then dowsed, played out the painful
cycle, the abyss you tried filling with clothes, the lies
you told of cancer, and the ways you painted
yourself battered by an innocent friend, though it was the drinks
that spilled you on your face, your eyes as abraded as the writing
you read in first editions. Funny how you liked the dark art

of other artists while your palette was turquoise and purple, an art
so bright and blended that you showed no pain
in the cafés, the beaches, the bodies you sketched. In writing
and drawing, your characters looked away as if what lay
in their eyes might have terrified or saved you. Cousin, you drank
the wrong potions. In your laughter, fiction, you painted

turquoise into people. Their black and white values were painted
lines, sharp definitions of what girls from wealthy families, whose art
brought fame, should do, and somehow, of that cruel bottle, you drank
as if your life depended on cruelty. Sure, you indulged yourself the pain
of your mother dropping dead when you were a teen, the lies
your father told to hide her affairs, but you didn't credit the right

amount for what you achieved: teaching, writing,
and painting. People on your street, in AA groups, came to paint
their lives blessed by your stories, knowing that so many lies
were woven into plots like Scheherazade's. Your telling was another art
they loved, but your stories didn't save you. Laughter mixed with pain
might have been the brew you could have drunk:

the draw was one of gratitude. Instead, recrimination was the drink
you guzzled after losing a husband, a career, and friends. Angry writing
in journals strewn in your unhinged house will not be your legacy. Pain
will not be what remains, I swear it. I swear on your paintings,
on the yard with apricots growing. I swear on the glass you artistically
arranged everywhere, I will not let our family associate you with lies

alone. What you drank was dark, but what you painted was turquoise,
what you wrote made priests into people, the perspective and art
of pain turned to watercolor, and your eyes blue with lies.

LANTERN

The whole summer I spread through shadows. Soft
tendrils snaked around twigs and flower stems until
October's clear blue voices called me out. Now ripe
and ridged, I give up rind and sweet seedy smell. With words
you slit eyes: you say you are not afraid of fullness. You carve
a nose for scents rising from a woman setting
another woman free, and you saw jagged teeth to
frighten and invite. Then you fill me with light,
and in the glow, I beckon other gay souls.

SOME SIGN

Katrina clients with children
and grannies and cousins
on one side of folding tables
and Red Cross volunteers from Missouri,
California, and Oregon on the other.
The room loud
with stories of water rising,
of strangers kind
with gasoline, of wallets
and eyeglasses and insulin
left behind.

One woman, white hair
shining, gaze set in the space
between us, tells me she lives
on the first floor, she just bought
her first bed ever, and the water rose
"to here, baby," she says, her hand
grazing her neck, the same sign
used for *stop* or *enough*, but
it was the wind, she says,
what scared her.

When it's time to sign a form
to get funds, her eyes fix just under
my eyes, and she asks, "Do you want me
to sign, or just use my mark?"

She holds the pen as if it were
a stick, the Red Cross form
the dirt where she digs.
To make the stick move
she bends as if in prayer. The mark

starts down from the right
diagonal to the left.
       One line.
The stick lifts
and it digs down from the left
      crossing over
           to the right.
She carves her name,
     her sign, her
        X.

SOMEPLACE SAFE

A girl, maybe twelve, behind me
tugging on my vest, her cheekbones
high, her eyes low, holds in her palm

a locked lock, white numbers
on black dial, no use against thieves
in the shelter. This black girl,
so silent, and I, so white,
both spinning and locked

in our combination, her need
to make things safe, my need
to make her safe. Her hand
rises higher as if height
makes the fear

of white girls in red vests
worth it, as if
the moon's strength mid-sky
is worth its rise.

                              Spin right, back

left, then right again,

the memory in my fingers
of how locks work, her hand
rising higher, her only way
to ask for help.
                              Right, left,

right,

she gives me *nineteen, five,*
thirty-eight, her only words,
and with a click, the lock
springs, she smiles, and we
spin, giggle, open wide.

SOMETHING TO WEAR

Triple X shirt, shoes bigger than Nikes worn
by pro-ball players, a muscle man struts
into the shelter. Freed from dank cell,
the convict said, "I won't leave this place
until I find my wife," and the word came
his wife didn't want to be found.

Clothes trucked from Connecticut
fit like sausage skin. Donated weights
under the one tree in the parking lot pumped
his rage. One-hundred-degree humidity,
clothes sopping, he paced the rim
of the indoor coliseum like a god
applauding lions before their kill.

Each day, white girl in red vest, I asked,
"Is there anything I can get you?"
Each day he said, "Get me my wife,"
but one day it was, "Get me a CD player."
And when I did, his head crowned
with ear phones, he was a singing king,
sweat dripping from his lips.

That evening we got him the PA system, and he
sang praise, "Jesus," he sang, "Jesus" and the thousands
in the coliseum rose to their feet, they sang, "Jesus"
in harmony, they said, "Sing it, baby," they said, "Amen,"
and the big man cried into the microphone, "Jesus" so bleak and
"Jesus" so sweet all of us believed we were clothed just right.

The Moon on the Tsunami

The moon
a month ago
made silver
the water swallowing
your shore.
You didn't want
to see dark things
floating
in hoary light, what
rooftop, what
scrap, what
limb. Too cruel
that fullness
pulling the tide.

Years ago
the woman I loved
on the other side
of an ocean wrote daily
notes to say the moon
she saw was the same one
I saw. Walking
under its thick light,
we were
inseparable.

After she
died, the moon
was all
I saw of her.

Tonight the full moon
is all flesh. Touch it

and you touch
what the ocean
took from you.

ANOTHER SUNSET WE SURVIVE

The bruise across the sky knots up, flares crimson,
streaking the underside of clouds with blood.

This sunset ignites the night my mother might die.
In ICU the drips slip into her veins, sticking her

to a life she'd rather let go. Already like a rope across
her palm, her life she'd release like rice tossed high,

deliberate. She wants to go big, avalanched by heart,
crushed in swift crash, not this simper of life seeping out,

tubes rubbing nostrils each night, the pause every second step
to lean against a wall. She'd wed death if she could, and I,

wretched daughter,
                              wish her wed. In each church I visit,
I clank coins into metal boxes and buy candles to kill her.

Sure, I pray for quick ends, but mostly, I can't stand
to face her, her fear suddenly tucked behind a smear

of smile when I enter the sterile room, the gray veins bulging
in her hand resting limp, the smoke inside her eyes, once

quick, coquettish, their light burning like this clotted sky.
This sunset keeps another night too damn alive.

kg

THIS SPRING

Kiss me like a killdeer cry, a broken wing
dragging ground to draw us from some
hurt we've borne. Kiss me blossom-soft,
clusters of cherry cups spilling light.

Kiss me two years after bombs dropped,
two years of men detained, made naked, piled
and plumbed, two years of bombs plundering
temples, pipelines, and four-year-olds praying.

Kiss me in rubble, the ocean god hungry
for flesh. I am hungry for you, no word
for *want* or *when*, the bone-knowing to go
deeper to sea when tsunamis roil.

In oil drilled from reindeer runs, in
diamonds turned drugs needled into boy-
arms, in prayers before the torsos are blown,
kiss me quick, kiss me deep, kiss me now.

In the dew of new moon, in the rise
of planting moon, the clouds strafing
the full moon as it sets, when the gibbous moon
dips into sunrise, kiss me then.

Kiss me when the blossoms take
the bombs, kiss me when the petals pool
in water clear of killing. In lenten light
please kiss, bless me now, bless us all.

ABOUT THE AUTHOR

Her sunrises are filled with golden retrievers and writing. Kate Gray's poems and stories chronicle her path on many rivers, some in Oregon, where she's lived for twenty years. Her chapbook, *Bone Knowing,* won the 2006 Gertrude poetry contest, and her first chapbook, *Where She Goes,* won the 2000 Blue Light Poetry Prize. She teaches at Clackamas College and is part of Portland's Dangerous Writing community.